ORIGAMI
PETS

Katie Gillespie

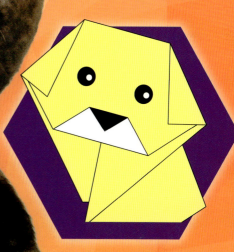

www.openlightbox.com

Step 1
Go to **www.openlightbox.com**

Step 2
Enter this unique code

YJAZVVGUJ

Step 3
Explore your interactive eBook!

CONTENTS

AV2 is optimized for use on any device

Your interactive eBook comes with...

Contents
Browse a live contents page to easily navigate through resources

Audio
Listen to sections of the book read aloud

Videos
Watch informative video clips

Weblinks
Gain additional information for research

Slideshows
View images and captions

Try This!
Complete activities and hands-on experiments

Key Words
Study vocabulary, and complete a matching word activity

Quizzes
Test your knowledge

Share
Share titles within your Learning Management System (LMS) or Library Circulation System

Citation
Create bibliographical references following the Chicago Manual of Style

This title is part of our AV2 digital subscription

1-Year K–5 Subscription
ISBN 978-1-7911-3320-7

Access hundreds of AV2 titles with our digital subscription.
Sign up for a FREE trial at **www.openlightbox.com/trial**

ORIGAMI
PETS

CONTENTS

Why Fold Origami?

Origami is the Japanese art of paper folding. The Japanese, and the Chinese before them, have been folding paper into different shapes and designs for hundreds of years. The term "origami" comes from the Japanese words *ori*, which means "folding," and *kami*, which means "paper."

Paper used to be very expensive, so origami was an activity that only the rich could afford. Over time, paper became less expensive, and more people were able to participate in origami. Today, it is an art form that anyone can enjoy.

It is fun to make objects out of paper. Before you start doing origami, there are three basic folds that you must learn. Knowing these three folds will help you create almost any simple origami model.

Hood Fold

Hood folds are often used to make an animal's head or neck. To make a hood fold, fold along the dotted line, and crease. Then, unfold the paper. Open the pocket you have created. Flip the paper inside out along the creases, and flatten.

Pocket Fold

Pocket folds are often used to make an animal's mouth or tail. To make a pocket fold, fold along the dotted line, and crease. Then, unfold the paper. Open the pocket you have created. Fold the point inside along the creases, and flatten.

Step Fold

Step folds are often used to make an animal's ears. To make a step fold, fold backward along the dotted line, and crease. Then, fold frontward along the dotted line and crease. Repeat as necessary.

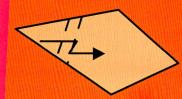

Pets

Owning a pet can be a great experience.
Pets are lovable and **loyal**. Most owners consider them to be important members of their family.

Having a pet is a big responsibility. When choosing a pet, it is important to understand the animal's needs and how much time it will take to care for it. Owners must commit to caring for their pet for life. That means taking time every day to feed, **groom**, play with, and clean up after it. Owners must be prepared to care for the pet when it is sick and to make sure it is trained properly.

As you fold the origami models in this book, think about how you would care for each animal. Which pet would you like to have in your home? Why?

Dogs are the **most popular pets** in the United States.

In 2021, Americans spent about **$44.2 billion** on **pet food and treats**.

About **90.5 million** U.S. families have pets.

What Is a Cat?

People have owned cats for thousands of years. Today, cats are one of the most popular pets in the world. In the United States, more than 40 million households have at least one cat.

House cats are related to big cats, such as the lion and tiger. Like big cats, house cats are good hunters. They use their sharp teeth and claws to catch **prey**, such as mice or birds.

Cats **communicate** in a variety of ways. A loud purr usually means that a cat is happy. A hissing cat is angry. If the tip of a cat's tail is twitching, the cat may be about to attack.

Eyes

Cats are known for having good eyesight. They can see much better at night than humans.

Body

Most cats grow to be about 28 inches (71 centimeters) long. This includes their body and their tail. Some cats grow to be much bigger. Cats have **agile** bodies. This helps them move quickly when hunting.

Tail

A cat's tail is part of its backbone. Cats use their tails for balance and to show their moods.

Ears

Cats can move their ears to locate sounds. Each ear can move **independently**.

Tongue

A cat's tongue is very rough. This is useful when a cat grooms itself. By licking its fur with its tongue, the cat is able to remove dirt and loose fur.

Paws

Cats have five toes on each of their front paws. Their back paws each have four toes. Cats have sharp claws on their paws. They use these claws to hunt their prey. Most cats can **retract** their claws when not in use.

How to Fold a Cat

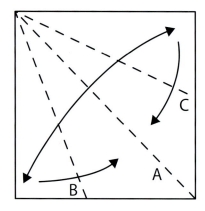

1 Fold in half along line A and crease. Open the paper. Then, fold along lines B and C to meet the center line, as shown.

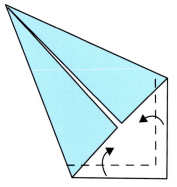

2 Fold along the right dotted line, as shown. Repeat on the bottom dotted line.

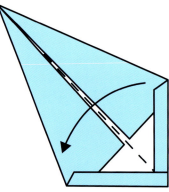

3 Fold in half lengthwise.

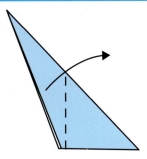

4 Fold the left side to the right along the dotted line, as shown.

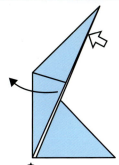

5 Open the pocket at the white arrow, and flatten at the star, as shown.

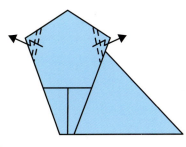

6 To make the cat's head, fold the bottom point inside along the dotted line, as shown.

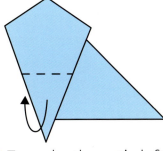

7 To make the cat's left ear, make a step fold on the left point, as shown. Repeat on the right side to make the cat's right ear.

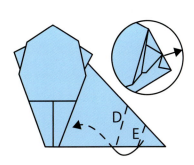

8 Make a pocket fold along line D. Then, to make the cat's tail, make a pocket fold along line E and pull out the tip, as shown.

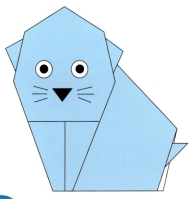

9 Finish the cat by drawing its eyes, nose, and whiskers.

What Is a Dog?

Humans have owned dogs as pets for at least 12,000 years. Dogs are well known for their loyalty. This is why they are sometimes called man's best friend.

People have come to rely on dogs in many ways. Some dogs have been taught to perform important jobs in society. Herding dogs are trained to help farmers look after livestock. Guard dogs are taught to protect homes and Seeing-eye dogs act as the eyes for people who are blind. Dogs can also be taught to help people in wheelchairs.

Eyes

Most dogs cannot see objects far away. Some dogs, however, can see movement from a long way away. Dogs can see color, but they do not see as many colors as humans.

Feet

Dogs are always walking on their toes. This is because the heel of their foot is raised and does not touch the ground. The bottom of each foot has touch pads. These help the dog absorb the shock from walking and running.

Ears

Dogs can hear four times the distance that humans can. They can hear higher-pitched sounds than humans. Each ear has more than 15 muscles that control its movements. These muscles allow the dog to raise, lower, and turn its ear flaps so that it can tell where a sound is coming from.

Whiskers

Dogs use the whiskers on their chin, muzzle, and cheeks to touch and feel their surroundings. Their whiskers are connected to nerves, which make them very sensitive.

Nose

Dogs rely on their sense of smell more than any other sense. Depending upon the **breed**, a dog's sense of smell is at least 10,000 times better than a human's and may be one million times better.

How to Fold a Dog

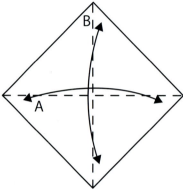

1 Fold in half along line A and crease. Open the paper. Then, fold in half along line B and crease. Open the paper.

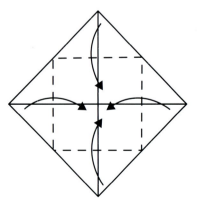

2 Fold the top point down to meet the center, as shown. Repeat on the bottom, left, and right points.

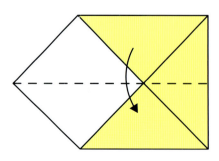

3 Open the left flap. Then, fold in half lengthwise along the dotted line.

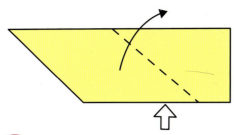

4 Open the pocket at the white arrow, and flatten.

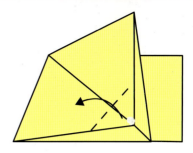

5 Fold the point along the dotted line, as shown.

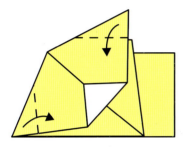

6 To make the dog's left ear, fold the left side in along the dotted line. Repeat on the right side to make the dog's right ear.

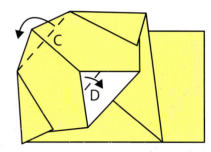

7 Fold the top point backward along line C, as shown. Then, fold down along line D to make the dog's nose.

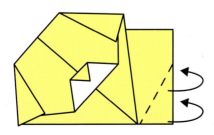

8 Fold backward along the dotted line, as shown.

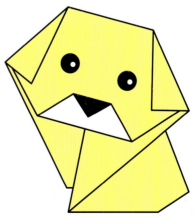

9 Finish the dog by turning it upright and drawing its eyes and nose.

What Is a Frog?

There are more than 4,000 kinds of frogs in the world. They are found on every continent, except Antarctica. Frogs are amphibians. This means they can live both in the water and on land. However, frogs cannot live in saltwater. They need fresh water to survive.

Frogs come in many shapes and sizes. Each type of frog behaves differently. Some frogs sit very still. They wait for food to come nearby. Others are very active and leap around their **environment**.

Skin

A frog's skin must be kept moist at all times. If its skin dries out, the frog will die. Frogs absorb water through their skin. This helps control their temperature. They can also take in air through their skin. This allows them to breathe, even when they are **hibernating**.

Legs

Frogs have long rear legs. Their front legs are much shorter. They help to prop the frog up when it sits. Frogs are some of the best leapers in the animal kingdom. Most frogs can jump as far as 20 times their own length.

Teeth

Frogs have teeth on their upper jaws, but the teeth are too weak to chew with. Instead, frogs use their teeth to hold prey before they swallow it whole.

Eyes

Frogs have bulging eyes, and they can see left, right, and behind their heads. Frogs have a membrane, or a thin layer of **tissue**, that covers their eyes. This protects them when they are underwater. Frogs can see partially through this membrane.

Tongue

Most frogs have long, sticky tongues. A frog uses its tongue to catch and swallow food. The tongue is attached to the front of the frog's mouth. This allows the tongue to stick out much farther than a human's.

How to Fold a Frog

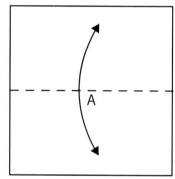

1 Fold in half along line A and crease. Open the paper.

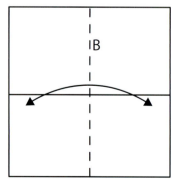

2 Fold in half along line B and crease. Open the paper.

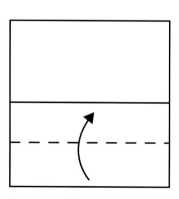

3 Fold the bottom up to meet the center line, as shown.

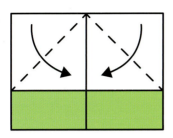

4 Fold the left point in to meet the center line, as shown. Repeat on the right point.

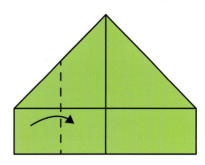

5 Fold the left side in to meet the center line.

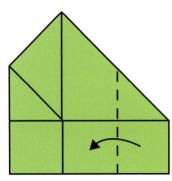

6 Fold the right side in to meet the center line.

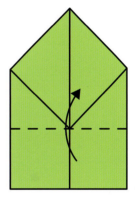

7 Fold the bottom up along the dotted line, as shown.

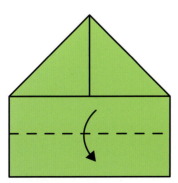

8 Fold down along the dotted line, as shown.

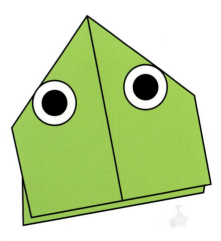

9 Finish the frog by turning it over and drawing its eyes.

What Is a Goldfish?

Many people keep fish as pets. The most common fish kept as a pet is the goldfish. Goldfish are not always gold in color. They can be red, orange, brown, gray, black, and even spotted. There are more than 125 varieties of goldfish.

Like all fish, goldfish must live in water to survive. Goldfish are coldwater fish. Goldfish can be kept in fishbowls, tanks, or even outdoor ponds. When goldfish are placed in bowls, the bowls need to be cleaned often. The best place to keep a goldfish is in an aquarium. There, the air and temperature can be controlled.

Eyes

A goldfish's eyes stay open all the time, even when it is sleeping. Goldfish see more colors than humans. This is because they can see **ultraviolet** and **infrared** light.

Teeth

Goldfish teeth are located in their throats. Goldfish use these teeth to crush and grind their food.

Gills

Water enters a goldfish's mouth and passes over the gills. The gills take oxygen from the water and release a gas called carbon dioxide. Then, the water exits through the gill openings. Gills allow the goldfish to live and breathe underwater.

Fins

A goldfish has five types of fins. The caudal fin is located at the end of its tail. When moved from side to side, it helps move the fish through water. Dorsal fins are found on the fish's back, and anal fins grow on its undersides. These fins help the fish stay upright. The pectoral and pelvic fins are located on each side of the fish. They help the fish stop and steer.

40

Some goldfish can live more than **40 years** in captivity.

Goldfish can survive in water as cool as

40° Fahrenheit

(4.5° Celsius).

How to Fold a Goldfish

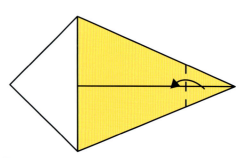

1 Fold in half along line A and crease. Open the paper. Then, fold in half along line B, and crease. Open the paper.

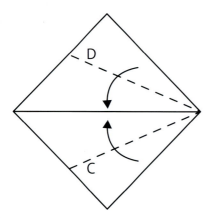

2 Fold along line C to meet the center line, as shown. Repeat for line D.

3 Fold the right point in along the dotted line, as shown.

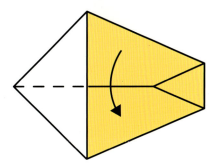

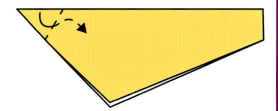

4 Fold in half lengthwise.

5 Make a pocket fold along the dotted line, as shown.

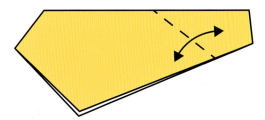

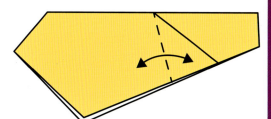

6 Fold forward along the dotted line, as shown, and crease. Unfold the paper.

7 Fold forward along the dotted line, as shown, and crease. Unfold the paper.

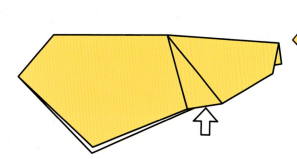

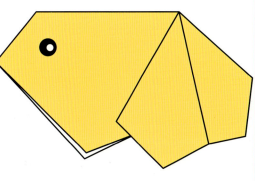

8 Open the pocket at the white arrow, and flatten.

9 Finish the goldfish by drawing its eye.

What Is a Hamster?

Hamsters are members of a large group of animals called rodents. Some types of hamsters have been around for centuries. The Syrian hamster was discovered in the deserts of Syria in the 1830s. By the 1940s, hamsters had become popular household pets.

While the Syrian hamster is the most common pet hamster, some people own other breeds. These include the Russian Dwarf, Chinese, and Roborovski hamsters. Each breed has its own unique features. However, all breeds share common traits. For instance, female hamsters, or sows, are larger than male hamsters. Male hamsters, or boars, live longer than female hamsters.

Mouth

A hamster has a large mouth, with 16 teeth. All hamsters have long upper and lower **incisors** at the front of their mouths. They also have **molars** on both sides of their mouths that help them chew food.

Paws and Feet

A hamster's front paws have four clawed toes. The front paws are used for grooming, digging, holding food, and emptying the cheek pouches. Hamsters have pads on the bottom of their feet. There are bumps on the pads which help them grip. Each foot has five toes.

Eyes

Hamsters have a poor sense of sight. They cannot see objects at close range. In addition, hamsters are nearly blind in bright daylight. They see best in dim light.

Cheeks

Hamsters have large pouches inside their cheeks. They use them to store and carry food. Hamsters can carry up to half their body weight inside their cheek pouches.

Nose

Hamsters have an excellent sense of smell. They use their noses as guides to identify many things, including food and other hamsters. If they are handled often, hamsters are even able to recognize their owners by their scent.

20

There are more than **20 species** of hamsters in the world.

A hamster's front teeth **never** stop growing.

How to Fold a Hamster

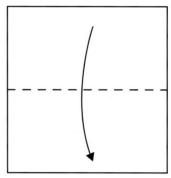

1 Fold in half along the dotted line, as shown.

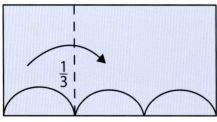

$\frac{1}{3}$

2 Fold the left side in one third, as shown.

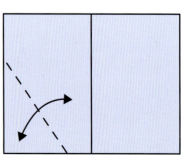

3 Fold along the dotted line, as shown, and crease. Unfold the paper.

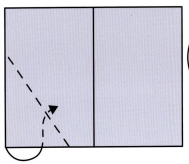 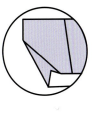 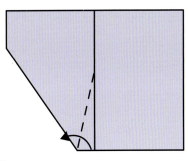

4 Make a pocket fold along the dotted line, as shown.

5 Fold along the dotted line, as shown.

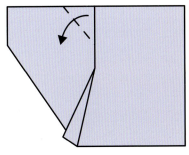 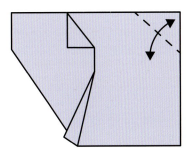

6 To make the hamster's ear, fold along the dotted line, as shown.

7 Fold along the dotted line, as shown, and crease. Unfold the paper.

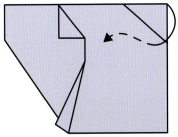 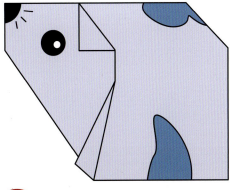

8 Make a pocket fold along the dotted line, as shown.

9 Finish the hamster by drawing its face and spots.

What Is a Rabbit?

Humans have kept rabbits as pets for hundreds of years. Rabbits are clean, smart, and quiet. They come in a wide variety of colors, shapes, sizes, and coats. There are 47 breeds of **domestic** rabbits around the world. Rabbits live for about nine years in nature. Pet rabbits usually live between 9 and 12 years.

Rabbits are very social animals. They get along well with humans and other animals. Most rabbits love to play and will often try to include their owners in their games. Rabbits also love to learn and can easily be trained to do many things.

Ears

On average, a rabbit's ears are 4 inches (10 cm) long. They can turn in any direction. A rabbit's ears also help regulate body temperature. The ears contain **blood vessels** that cool the rabbit when it becomes hot.

Legs

Rabbits have long hind legs and short front legs. When a rabbit runs, its hind legs touch the ground before its front legs. Rabbits will stomp their back feet when they are scared. They do this to warn other rabbits about danger.

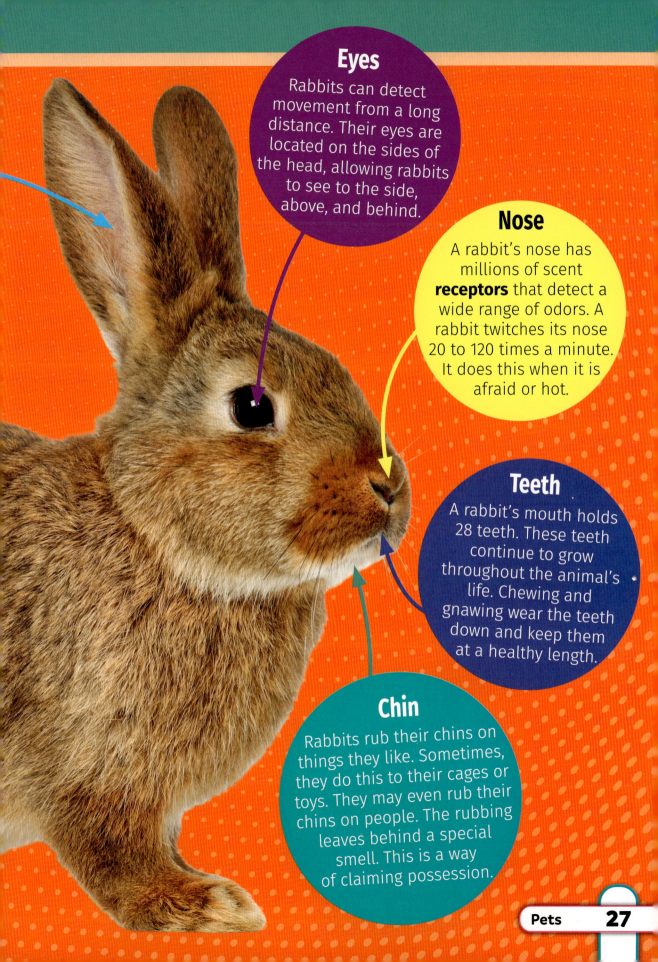

Eyes

Rabbits can detect movement from a long distance. Their eyes are located on the sides of the head, allowing rabbits to see to the side, above, and behind.

Nose

A rabbit's nose has millions of scent **receptors** that detect a wide range of odors. A rabbit twitches its nose 20 to 120 times a minute. It does this when it is afraid or hot.

Teeth

A rabbit's mouth holds 28 teeth. These teeth continue to grow throughout the animal's life. Chewing and gnawing wear the teeth down and keep them at a healthy length.

Chin

Rabbits rub their chins on things they like. Sometimes, they do this to their cages or toys. They may even rub their chins on people. The rubbing leaves behind a special smell. This is a way of claiming possession.

How to Fold a Rabbit

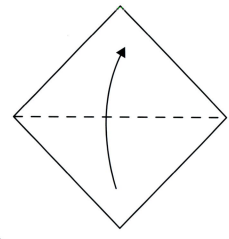

1 Fold in half along the dotted line, as shown.

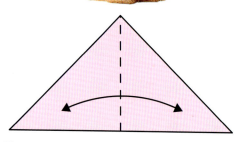

2 Fold in half along the dotted line, as shown, and crease. Open the paper.

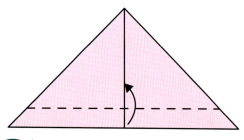

3 Fold the bottom up along the dotted line, as shown.

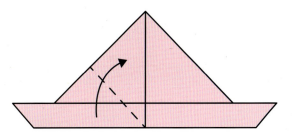

4 Fold the left side in to meet the center line, as shown.

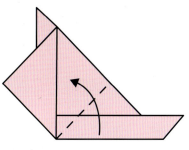

5 Fold the right side in to meet the center line, as shown.

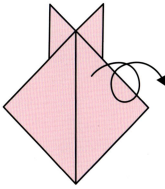

6 Turn the rabbit over.

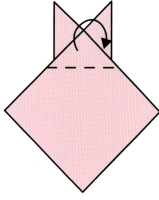

7 Fold the top point backward along the dotted line, as shown.

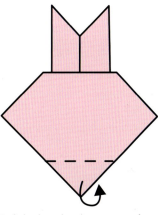

8 Fold the bottom point backward along the dotted line, as shown.

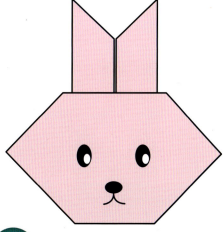

9 Finish the rabbit by drawing its face.

Quiz

1
How many toes do cats have on each of their front paws?

2
Why are dogs' whiskers very sensitive?

3
What kind of animal is a frog?

5
What do hamsters use their cheek pouches for?

4
Where are a goldfish's teeth located?

6
How long are an average rabbit's ears?

ANSWERS

1. Five 2. Because they are connected to nerves 3. An amphibian 4. In its throat 5. To store and carry food 6. 4 inches (10 cm) long

Key Words

agile: able to move quickly and easily

blood vessels: any of the tubes in the body through which blood flows

breed: particular type of animal

communicate: to exchange information

domestic: not wild, tame

environment: the living things and conditions of a particular place

groom: make neat and pleasant in appearance

hibernating: being inactive during the winter

incisors: front teeth used for cutting, tearing, or chewing

independently: free from the control of others

infrared: light that is invisible to the human eye, characterized by long wavelengths

loyal: showing strong and lasting support for something

molars: broad teeth used for grinding

prey: animals that are hunted for food

receptors: sensitive nerve endings

retract: to draw back in

tissue: a group of cells in a plant or animal that are similar in form

ultraviolet: light that is invisible to the human eye, characterized by short wavelengths

Index

Get the best of both worlds.

AV2 bridges the gap between print and digital.

The expandable resources toolbar enables quick access to content including **videos**, **audio**, **activities**, **weblinks**, **slideshows**, **quizzes**, and **key words**.

Animated videos make static images come alive.

Resource icons on each page help readers to further **explore key concepts**.

Published by Lightbox Learning Inc.
276 5th Avenue
Suite 704 #917
New York, NY 10001
Website: www.openlightbox.com

Library of Congress Cataloging-in-Publication Data available upon request.

ISBN 978-1-7911-4449-4 (hardcover)
ISBN 978-1-7911-4450-0 (softcover)
ISBN 978-1-7911-4451-7 (multi-user eBook)

Printed in Guangzhou, China
1 2 3 4 5 6 7 8 9 0 26 25 24 23 22

022022
101321

Designer: Ana María Vidal   Project Coordinator: Sara Cucini

Every reasonable effort has been made to trace ownership and to obtain permission to reprint copyright material. The publisher would be pleased to have any errors or omissions brought to its attention so that they may be corrected in subsequent printings.

The publisher acknowledges Getty Images and Shutterstock as the primary image suppliers for this title.